ALL THE WAY TO THE TOP

How One Girl's Fight for Americans with Disabilities Changed Everything

words by Annette Bay Pimentel

pictures by Nabi H. Ali

foreword by Jennifer Keelan-Chaffins

Sourcebooks eXplore

FOREWORD

by Jennifer Keelan-Chaffins

I was born with cerebral palsy, which means that I use a wheelchair to help me get around every day. From a young age, I learned that buses, museums, libraries, and even schools that were accessible to my able-bodied peers were not accessible to me because there were no wheelchair ramps. Imagine not being able to join in with your friends because you can't get into the building where they're meeting! I felt left out and did not like being separated from everyone, especially my younger sister, Kailee. As my family and I realized that people with disabilities were not treated as equally as able-bodied people, we decided to join the disability rights movement to help change things for the better.

I participated in my very first protest in Phoenix, Arizona, in 1987 when I was six years old. This was the first time I saw other people with disabilities protesting for their right to be recognized as equals. At first, I didn't know quite what to think, but after carefully observing the adults at this protest, both my sister and I realized that people with disabilities had the right to be treated like everyone else, and that Kailee and I did not have to be separated.

As one of the very few young children who got to be closely involved in the disability rights movement, I recognized that I had a very important responsibility placed upon me. I wasn't just representing myself, I was also representing my generation and future generations of children with disabilities who also felt left out as they struggled for the same rights as everyone else.

It was this responsibility that led me to participate in a big protest called the Capitol Crawl, a decision that a lot of people say helped convince Congress to pass an important law for the disability rights movement: the Americans with Disabilities Act. I hope that by sharing my story, kids everywhere will see that you don't have to be a grown-up to make a difference. If you believe in something, say it loud for everyone to hear! The passing of the Americans with Disabilities Act was a big win for the disability rights movement. But we still have a long way to go, and I keep using my voice to speak up for what I think is right. You can too!

Jennifer Keelan may be small, but her voice is mighty. "Yee-haw!"

Snowball responds, speeding up from a walk to a trot. Jennifer loves to go fast! But she knows she'll soon have less time for riding since she's finally old enough for school. She can't wait to make new friends.

She's ready to **GO!**

The school's not far. Jennifer rolls outside, down the sidewalk, to the corner.

But... **STOP!**

A four-inch curb is a cliff to someone who uses a wheelchair.

Her Grandpa eases her wheelchair over the curb. Though the drop jolts Jennifer, she makes it to the building.

But... **STOP!**

The school says Jennifer doesn't belong there because she uses a wheelchair.

Instead, Jennifer and her mom find a different school that says she can attend kindergarten, but only for part of the afternoon, when lunch is over. As Jennifer rolls in each day, everyone is already busy. She has to figure out what's going on and how to join in.

Since most kids have never met someone who uses a wheelchair, her classmates are confused and even a little afraid.

"You'll never be one of us," some of them say.

Jennifer knows they're wrong. She's just a friend waiting to happen! But how do you change someone's mind? She's not sure, but she's not about to give up.

Jennifer and her family hear about activists who are working to make sure people with disabilities have access to public places, like schools. They want to know more, so they attend a strategy meeting. Jennifer has never seen anything like it! The room is full of grown-ups with all sorts of disabilities. Some use wheelchairs. Some use canes. None of them are sitting around waiting for things to change. They're shouting, laughing, and planning a big protest to get wheelchair lifts on buses.

They turn to Jennifer.
"Do you want to come?"

Yes! She wants to **GO!**

Downtown, Jennifer rolls to the microphone and tells her story. She leads marchers through the streets, chanting, "The people united will never be defeated!"

It feels good to speak up for what she believes in. She can't wait to do it again.

She's raring to **GO!**

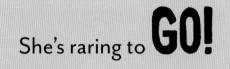

She protests in Phoenix,

rolls through streets in San Francisco,

waves signs in Montreal.

The demonstrations don't always change people's minds, but Jennifer is used to that.

Even when her
neighborhood school
finally agrees she
can attend, she and
her classmates with
disabilities aren't allowed
to eat in the cafeteria with
everyone else. That hurts,
but she keeps going.

Working with other activists revs her up. Yet she can't help noticing that she and her sister are usually the only kids out there raising their voices. Still, she can't leave all the protesting to grown-ups. She knows firsthand that children with disabilities get ignored too. So she keeps speaking up.

When Jennifer is eight, activists propose a new law called the Americans with Disabilities Act, or ADA. The law insists schools, governments, and businesses make room for all people, including those with disabilities. Jennifer feels like dancing! If it passes, it means sidewalks with curb cuts, buildings with ramps in addition to steps, and elevators with braille panels. It means Jennifer and her classmates with disabilities can finally go to the cafeteria with everyone else for lunch.

Jennifer and her family watch the news for updates on the ADA, but reporters never mention it. She switches off the TV in frustration, wishing she could change reporters' minds on what's worth talking about.

Instead, the Keelans get their updates about the ADA when activist friends call. It's bad news. Members of Congress say the law will be too complicated and too expensive. They say it's just not worth it.

Since the news station is ignoring people with disabilities, Jennifer and her friends are determined to find another way to make Congress hear their voices.

It's **GO** time!

Her family buys plane tickets to Washington, DC.

As they march down Pennsylvania Avenue, Jennifer has never shouted louder.

"What do we want?"

"THE ADA!"

"When do we want it?"

"NOW!"

Finally, they reach the U.S. Capitol. But...**STOP!**

A mountain of steps block Jennifer and other people using wheelchairs from the building where Congress makes laws.

Grown-ups slide out of their wheelchairs and start pulling themselves up the steps. They will make sure members of Congress know they are here.

Jennifer's heart races. This is what she has been shouting about! "I want to climb the steps," she says.

But...**STOP!**

The grown-ups think she's too young. "You can't do it."

Jennifer knows this is not just about her. It's about her friends at school who were shut out of the cafeteria at lunch. It's about millions of other kids she's never met who get **STOPPED** at every turn. Jennifer wants to speak up for all the kids with disabilities who aren't there.

"I NEED TO CLIMB THE STEPS."

She slides out of her wheelchair, scoots along the sidewalk to the bottom of the stairway, and puts her hands on the first step. She hauls herself up. Tiny bits of dirt and rock dig into her skin. She drags herself up another step.

The crowd roars. Reporters surround her with cameras and microphones, recording her gutsy climb.

"I'll take all night if I have to," she vows. And she keeps heaving...hauling...dragging herself up those steps.

She keeps **GOING...**

ALL THE WAY TO THE TOP.

Handicapped Stage
Crawl-In Protest Up
Steps of Capitol

Legislation Attac

Pictures of Jennifer climbing the steps flash around the world. Reporters start talking about the ADA. Members of Congress see the news, listen to the activists, and, finally, **PASS THE ADA!**

Laws like the ADA don't change things overnight. Entrances have to be rebuilt, sidewalks redesigned, buses reengineered. Slowest of all, minds have to change. So Jennifer will continue shouting and waving signs, organizing and explaining. She will continue fighting for what she knows is right.

Jennifer has places to GO...

AND NOTHING WILL STOP HER NOW.

THE ROAD TO THE TOP

WHAT IS A DISABILITY?

A disability is a physical, mental, or emotional condition that limits how a person can move or sense the world or do daily activities. Some disabilities are obvious, like stuttering or needing a wheelchair or guide dog. Other disabilities, like hearing loss or social anxiety, are not as visible but can be just as life changing.

FIGHTING FOR RIGHTS

Disability rights activists work to make sure people with disabilities can participate in everyday life. Like civil rights and women's rights activists, they often use nonviolent demonstrations to call attention to problems and encourage change.

YOU CAN'T CATCH CEREBRAL PALSY

Jennifer Keelan-Chaffins's disabilities were caused by cerebral palsy, or CP. CP is damage to the part of the brain that controls movement. The damage from CP happens either before a baby is born or during birth. So you can't catch CP like you catch a cold! Not everyone with CP has the same disability. Some people with CP can't move at all while others may have barely noticeable disabilities, like weakness on one side of the body.

ACCESS FOR EVERYONE

When you have a physical disability that requires you to use assistive devices like a wheelchair or a walker, it can be difficult to get around. Stairs without ramps, narrow bathroom stalls, and sidewalks without curb cuts all pose problems. Activists used the Capitol Crawl to demonstrate these barriers and to pressure lawmakers to pass legislation to make public spaces more accessible.

PROBLEM OR PERSON?

While physical barriers pose challenges to people with disabilities, social attitudes can be even more frustrating. People may focus on a disability as a problem to be solved instead of paying attention to the person with the disability. Or people with disabilities may be treated with low expectations, as if having a disability means they are incapable. On the other hand, people with disabilities are sometimes treated as heroes simply for doing everyday things when they just want to live their lives.

"WE WILL RIDE!"

In 1983, Rev. Wade Blank and nineteen people who used wheelchairs formed a group, ADAPT, to fight for wheelchair lifts on city buses in Denver, Colorado. The Gang of Nineteen shouted, "We will ride!" and rolled their wheelchairs onto the road to stop city buses from moving. ADAPT's protest changed the way reporters and lawmakers in Colorado thought about people with disabilities. It also paved the way for other demonstrations, including the Capitol Crawl, which focused attention all over the world on disability rights issues. Jennifer's first protest was planned by ADAPT, and she learned how to be an activist from adults in the group.

A LAW FOR EVERYONE

The Americans with Disabilities Act, or ADA, protects people with all sorts of disabilities: physical, mental, and emotional. Because of the ADA, public buildings have ramps as well as steps, elevators have braille panels, and TVs have closed captioning. The ADA supports the efforts of people with disabilities to go to school, to compete for jobs, and to live independently. This is what Jennifer and her fellow protesters were fighting for at the Capitol Crawl.

THE CAPITOL CRAWL

The Capitol Crawl was a demonstration designed to convince lawmakers to pass the ADA by showing them how difficult it was for people with physical disabilities to move around in public spaces. The dramatic crawl up the Capitol steps was planned in secret. Adult planners told Jennifer she shouldn't do the climb. They worried both that it would be too difficult for a child, and that people watching her would assume adults with disabilities are childlike. But Jennifer wanted to represent kids with disabilities. That day, Rev. Wade Blank advised her, "Do what is in your heart." So she climbed.

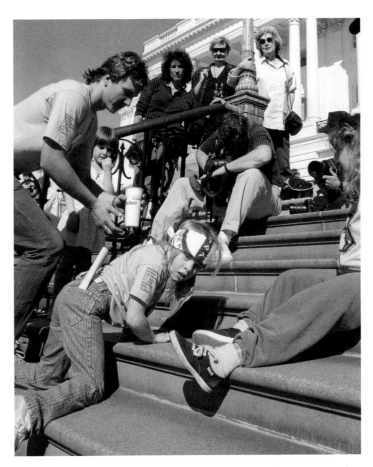

March 12, 1990—Jennifer Keelan, left, joins the disability rights activists as they crawl up the steps of the U.S. Capitol in Washington to draw support for the proposed bill. The group of about one thousand people rode in wheelchairs down Pennsylvania Avenue from the White House to the Capitol.

HELP WANTED: ACTIVISTS

When activists see something unfair happening, they take action to fix it. There's no minimum age to become an activist! Jennifer started speaking up for people with disabilities when she was six years old. Anyone can choose to become an activist, no matter your age. All you have to do is use your voice! Start by talking to others about what matters to you. You have the ability to create change, whether it's nudging the world in a new direction or creating international news like Jennifer!

LIFE BEFORE AND AFTER THE ADA

When doctors diagnosed Jennifer Keelan with cerebral palsy, they told her mom she should send Jennifer away to live somewhere else. For many years, this had been common advice. Many children with disabilities were separated from their families and sent to live in public hospitals. Jennifer's family wouldn't hear of it, though. They kept Jennifer home and focused on the things she could do, like ride horses.

Jennifer and her family were thrilled when the ADA passed. They were glad to have the law on the side of including people with disabilities in everyday life. But change is slow. Many people had never met someone with disabilities and were frightened. Sometimes parents wouldn't let their children play with or speak to Jennifer because of her disability. All through Jennifer's school years, even after the ADA became law, the Keelans struggled to get Jennifer into classes based on her educational needs and not on assumptions about her disability. Eventually she dropped out of school, got her GED, and completed a college degree online.

The ADA has been law for thirty years, but the fight for disability rights continues. Jennifer, alongside many other people who use assistive devices, continues to find public places that are not wheelchair accessible. She struggles to find accessible housing. So she is still an activist. She encourages governments and businesses to follow federal law as laid out in the ADA, and she works to make sure local laws and policies give all people—including those with disabilities—access to the community and opportunities to be contributing citizens. Jennifer isn't about to give up. She will continue to raise her voice to fight for what's right!

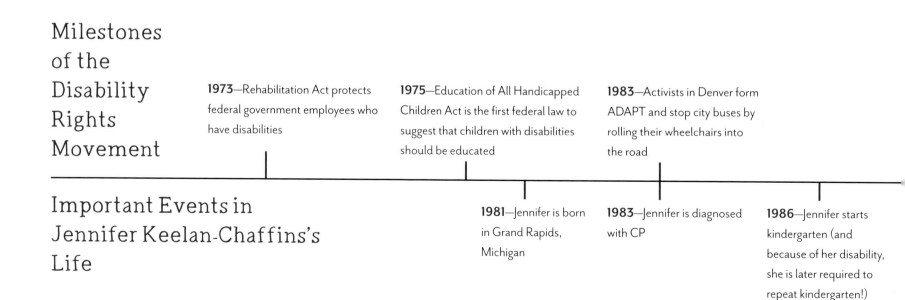

Milestones
of the
Disability
Rights
Movement

1973—Rehabilitation Act protects federal government employees who have disabilities

1975—Education of All Handicapped Children Act is the first federal law to suggest that children with disabilities should be educated

1983—Activists in Denver form ADAPT and stop city buses by rolling their wheelchairs into the road

Important Events in
Jennifer Keelan-Chaffins's
Life

1981—Jennifer is born in Grand Rapids, Michigan

1983—Jennifer is diagnosed with CP

1986—Jennifer starts kindergarten (and because of her disability, she is later required to repeat kindergarten!)

BIBLIOGRAPHY

Eaton, William J. "Disabled Persons Rally, Crawl Up Capitol Steps." *Los Angeles Times*, March 13, 1990. http://lat.ms/2plj5lC.

Gilkey, Alison. *Lives Worth Living*. Documentary film, YouTube video, originally broadcast by PBS. Directed by Eric Neudel. Natick, MA: Storyline Motion Pictures & Independent Television Service, 2011. https://www.youtube.com/watch?v=Kqea96RdLdI.

Harkin, Tom. "Americans with Disabilities Act at 20: A Nation Transformed." *Huffington Post*, July 26, 2010. http://huff.to/2q6FbFX.

It's Our Story. "Jennifer Keelan, 01–12." YouTube video series. July 21, 2010. https://bit.ly/2Uqug7p.

Keelan, Cyndi. Mother. Telephone interviews with author. May 9, 2017; October 4, 2018.

Keelan-Chaffins, Jennifer. Telephone interviews and email correspondence with author. May 9, 2017; August 5, 2018; October 4, 2018.

"The Little Girl Who Crawled Up the Capitol Steps 25 Years Later: Jennifer Keelan and the ADA." *CP Daily Living*, July 24, 2015. http://bit.ly/2qslJoM.

Michaels, Samantha. "The Americans with Disabilities Act Is Turning 25. Watch the Dramatic Protest That Made It Happen." *Mother Jones*, July 25, 2015. http://bit.ly/1HR24QB.

Winter, Michael. "1990 – Washington – Michael Winter." ADAPT, April 30, 2017. http://bit.ly/2qsLw1r.

All direct quotations came from Jennifer Keelan-Chaffins and It's Our Story, Video 8.

1988—Gallaudet University students force a change of college president with their "Deaf President Now" campaign

1990—Frustrated by the slow progress on the ADA, disability rights activists march on Washington, DC, culminating in the Capitol Crawl

The Fair Housing Act of 1968 is amended to provide some protection for people with disabilities

1989—Lawmakers draft the Americans with Disabilities Act and begin debating it

Congress passes the ADA and Pres. George H. W. Bush signs it into law on July 26, 1990

2008—Congress passes amendments to the ADA to restore protections that court rulings had removed

1987—Jennifer participates in her first protest, demonstrating for wheelchair lifts on buses

1988—Jennifer is arrested at a disability rights protest in Montreal

1990—Jennifer participates in the Capitol Crawl, bringing media attention to disability rights and the ADA

2017—Jennifer graduates from Arizona State University

To Mahdia, for looking out for all of us.

—NHA

Text © 2020 by Annette Bay Pimentel
Illustrations © 2020 by Nabi H. Ali
Internal image © AP Photos, Jeff Markowitz
Cover and internal design © 2020 by Sourcebooks

The full color art was first sketched, then painted digitally in Procreate.

Published by Sourcebooks eXplore, an imprint of Sourcebooks Kids
P.O. Box 4410, Naperville, Illinois 60567-4410
(630) 961-3900
sourcebookskids.com

Library of Congress Cataloging-in-Publication Data is on file with the publisher.

Source of Production: Leo Paper, Heshan City, Guangdong Province, China
Date of Production: January 2023
Run Number: 5030503

Printed and bound in China.

LEO 10 9